Antonín DVOŘÁK

SLAVONIC RHAPSODIES
Op. 45 / B. 86
(1878)

Study Score
Partitur

PETRUCCI LIBRARY PRESS

ORCHESTRA

2 Flutes (also Piccolo - No.3)
Piccolo (No.1)
2 Oboes
2 Clarinets
2 Bassoons

4 Horns
2 Trumpets
3 Trombones

Timpani
Triangle
Cymbals / Bass Drum
Harp

Violins I
Violins II
Violas
Violoncellos
Double Basses

Duration: ca. 40 minutes

First performance (Nos.1 and 2): November 17, 1878
Prague, National Theatre
National Theatre Orchestra / Composer

First performance (No.3): September 24, 1879
Berlin, Orchestra / Wilhelm Taubert

ISBN: 978-1-60874-143-4
This score is a slightly modified unabridged reprint of the score
issued in 1959 by the Czech state publisher SNKLHU, plate H. 2818.
The score has been scaled to fit the present format.

Printed in the USA
First Printing: October, 2015

SLAVONIC RHAPSODIES
Op. 45 / B. 86

I

19. II. 1878

Antonín Dvořák (1841-1904)
Edited by Antonín Pokorný and Karel Šolc

4

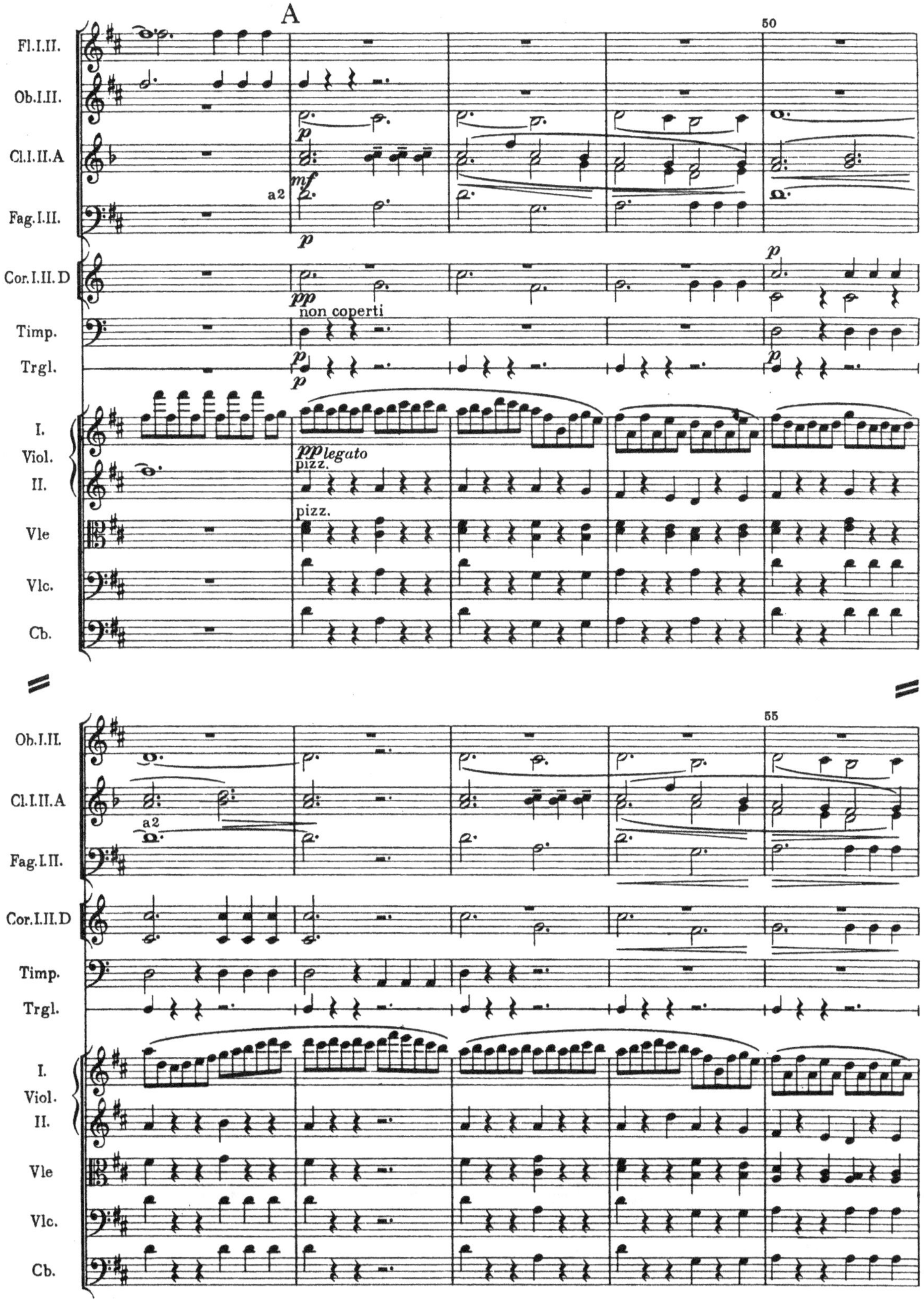
A
50
Fl.I.II.
Ob.I.II.
Cl.I.II.A
Fag.I.II.
Cor.I.II.D
Timp.
Trgl.
I.
Viol.
II.
Vle
Vlc.
Cb.
a2
p
mf
pp
non coperti
pp legato
pizz.
pizz.
55
Ob.I.II.
Cl.I.II.A
Fag.I.II.
Cor.I.II.D
Timp.
Trgl.
I.
Viol.
II.
Vle
Vlc.
Cb.
a2

12

14

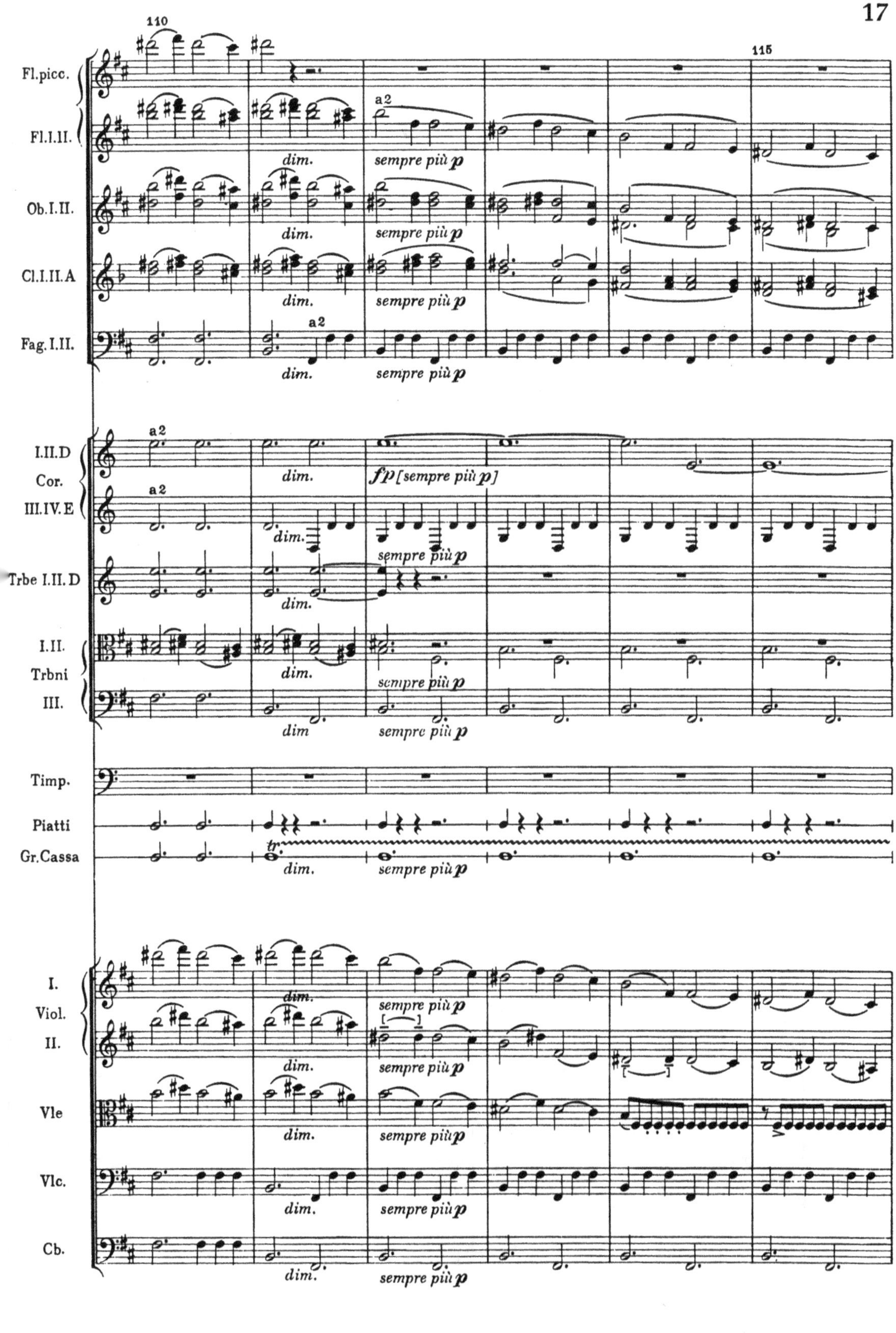
110
115
Fl.picc.
Fl.I.II.
Ob.I.II.
Cl.I.II.A
Fag.I.II.
a2
dim.
sempre più p
I.II.D
Cor.
III.IV.E
fp [sempre più p]
Trbe I.II.D
I.II.
Trbni
III.
dim
Timp.
Piatti
Gr.Cassa
tr
I.
Viol.
II.
Vle
Vlc.
Cb.

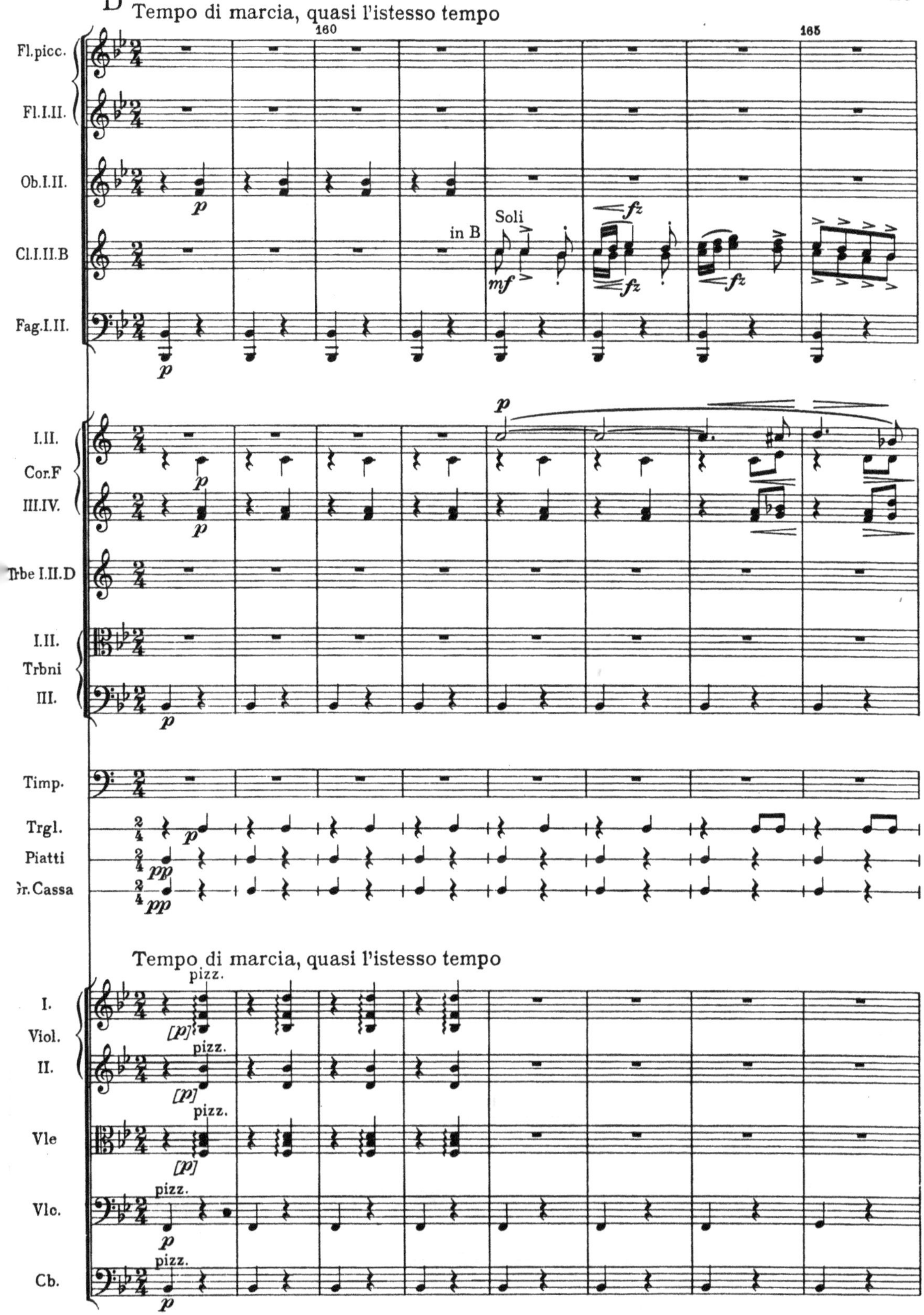
D
Tempo di marcia, quasi l'istesso tempo
160
165
Fl.picc.
Fl.I.II.
Ob.I.II.
Cl.I.II.B
in B
Soli
Fag.I.II.
I.II.
Cor.F
III.IV.
Trbe I.II.D
I.II.
Trbni
III.
Timp.
Trgl.
Piatti
Gr.Cassa
Tempo di marcia, quasi l'istesso tempo
pizz.
I.
Viol.
II.
Vle
Vlc.
Cb.

30

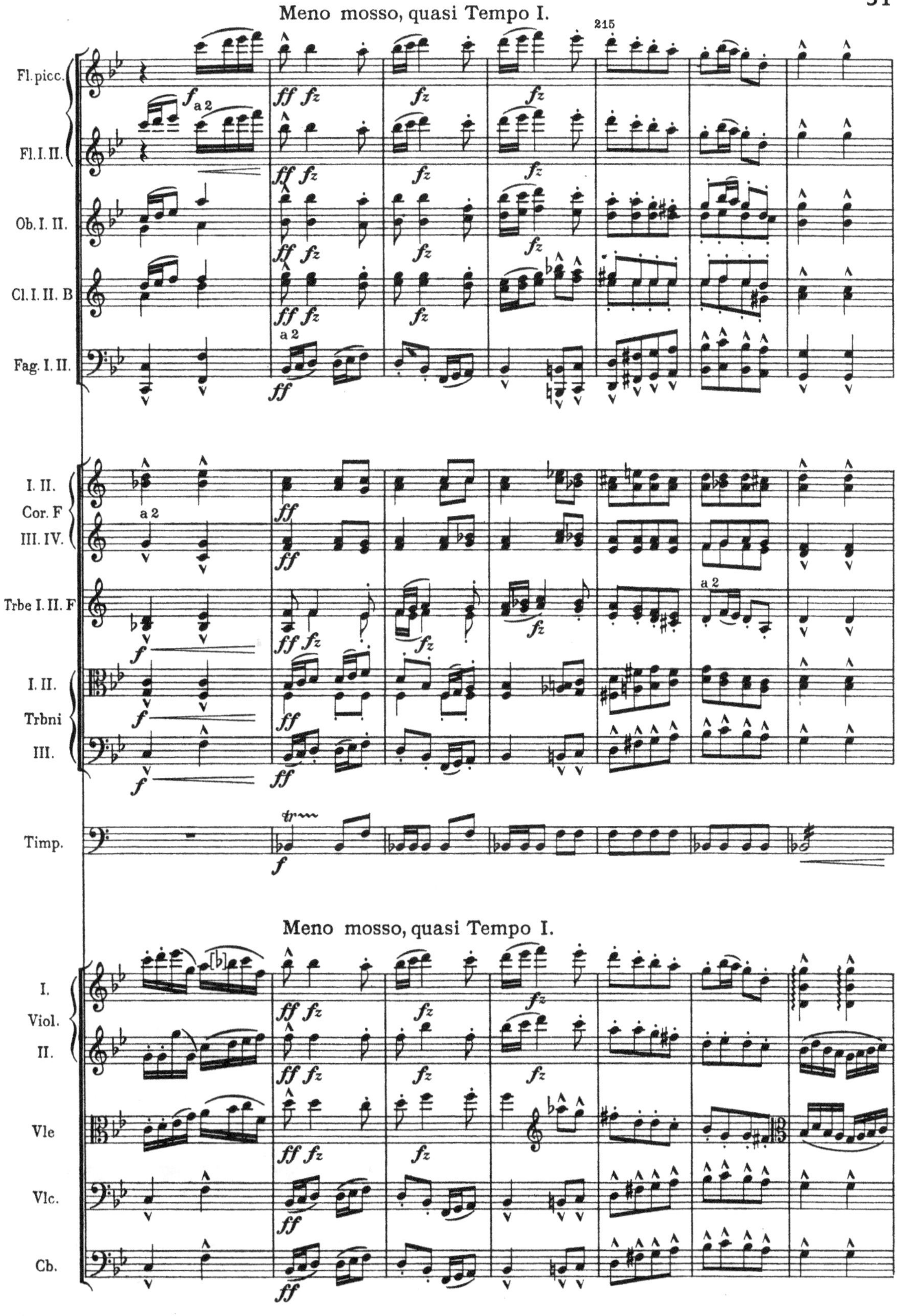
Meno mosso, quasi Tempo I.
215
Fl. picc.
Fl. I. II.
Ob. I. II.
Cl. I. II. B
Fag. I. II.
I. II.
Cor. F
III. IV.
Trbe I. II. F
I. II.
Trbni
III.
Timp.
Meno mosso, quasi Tempo I.
I.
Viol.
II.
Vle
Vlc.
Cb.

38

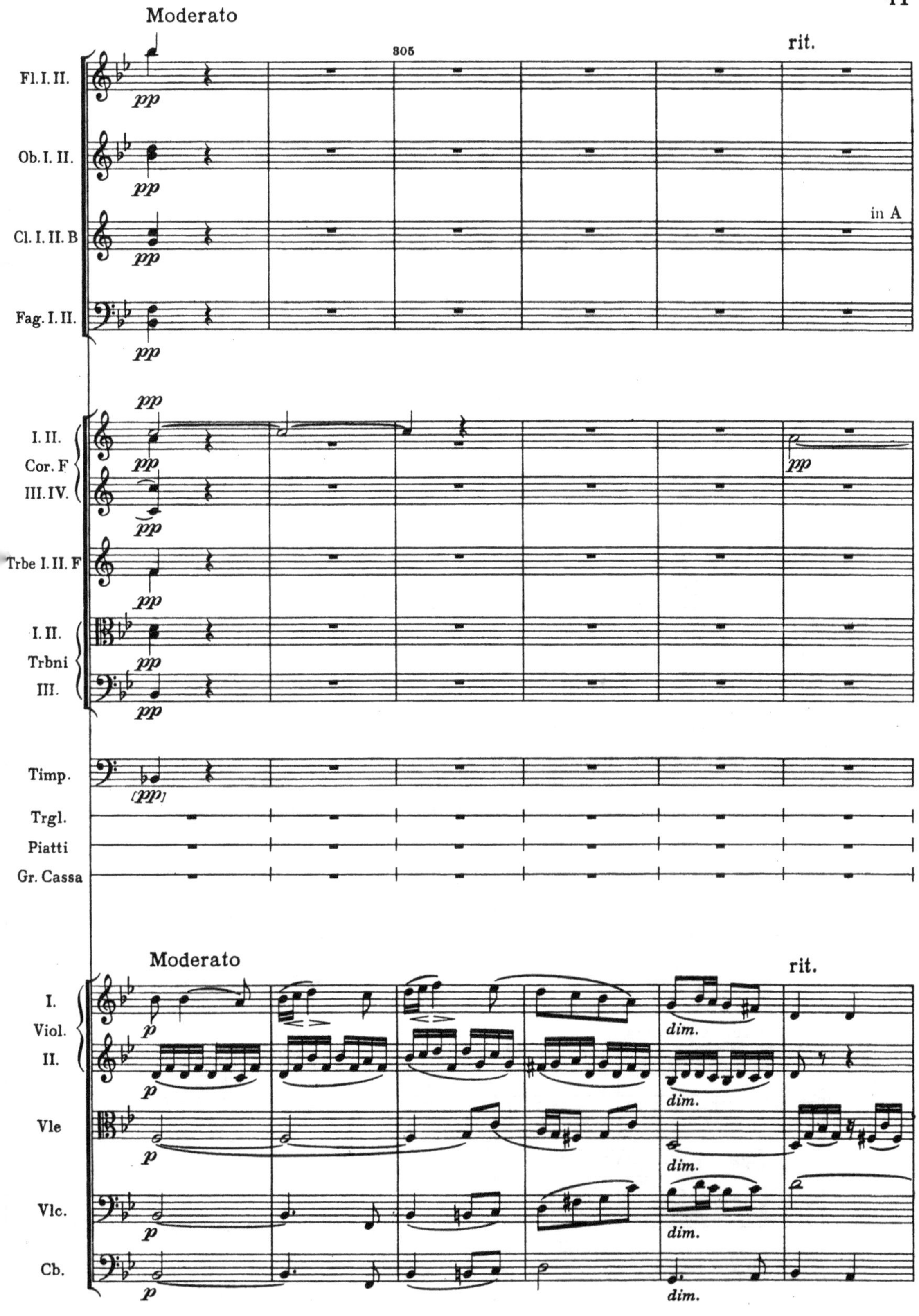
Moderato
305
rit.
Fl. I. II.
Ob. I. II.
Cl. I. II. B
in A
Fag. I. II.
I. II.
Cor. F
III. IV.
Trbe I. II. F
I. II.
Trbni
III.
Timp.
Trgl.
Piatti
Gr. Cassa
Moderato
rit.
I.
Viol.
II.
Vle
Vlc.
Cb.
dim.

46

48

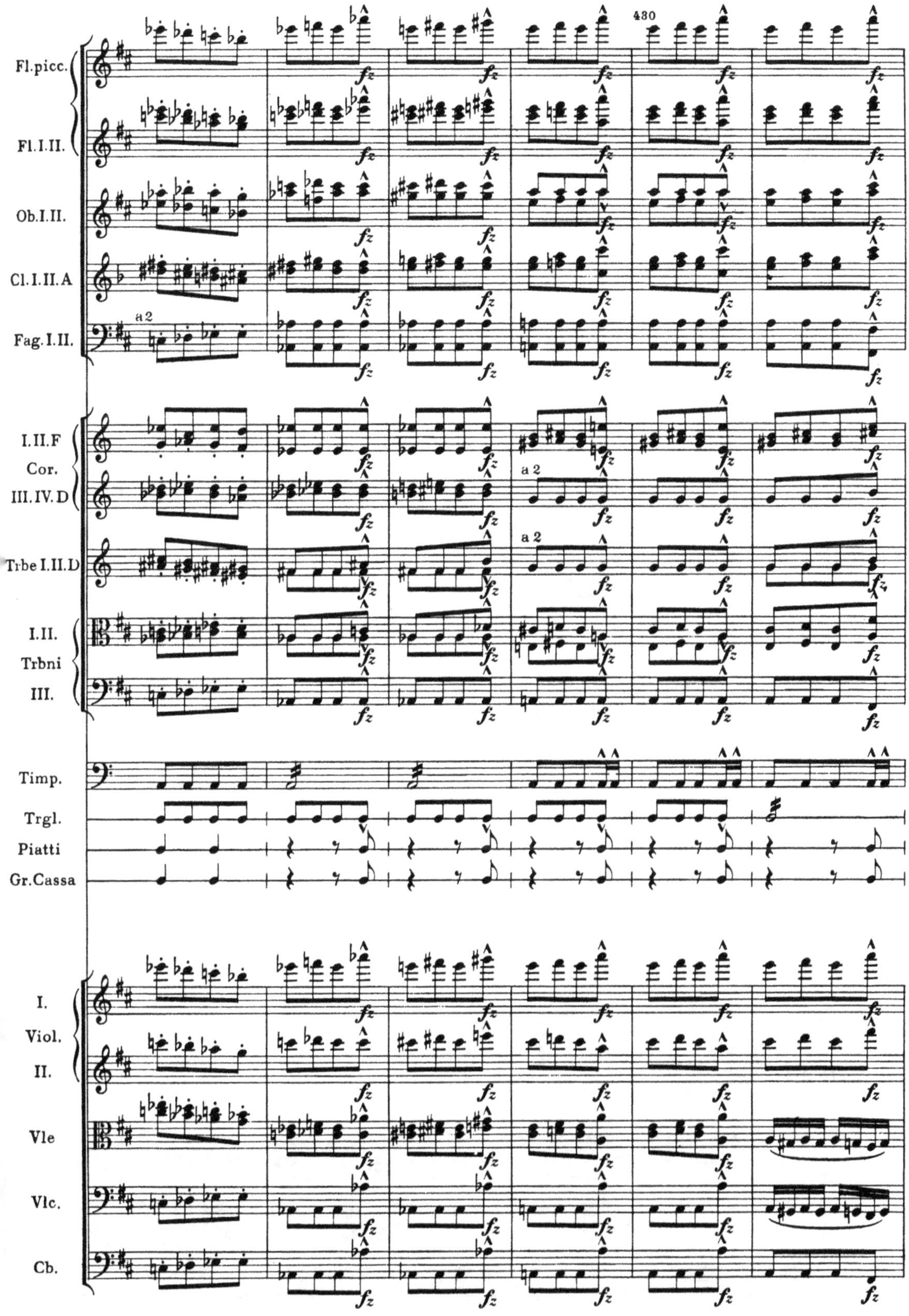
480
Fl.picc.
Fl.I.II.
Ob.I.II.
Cl.I.II.A
Fag.I.II.
a 2
I.II.F
Cor.
III.IV.D
a 2
Trbe I.II.D
a 2
I.II.
Trbni
III.
Timp.
Trgl.
Piatti
Gr.Cassa
I.
Viol.
II.
Vle
Vlc.
Cb.
fz

70

II

78

79

82

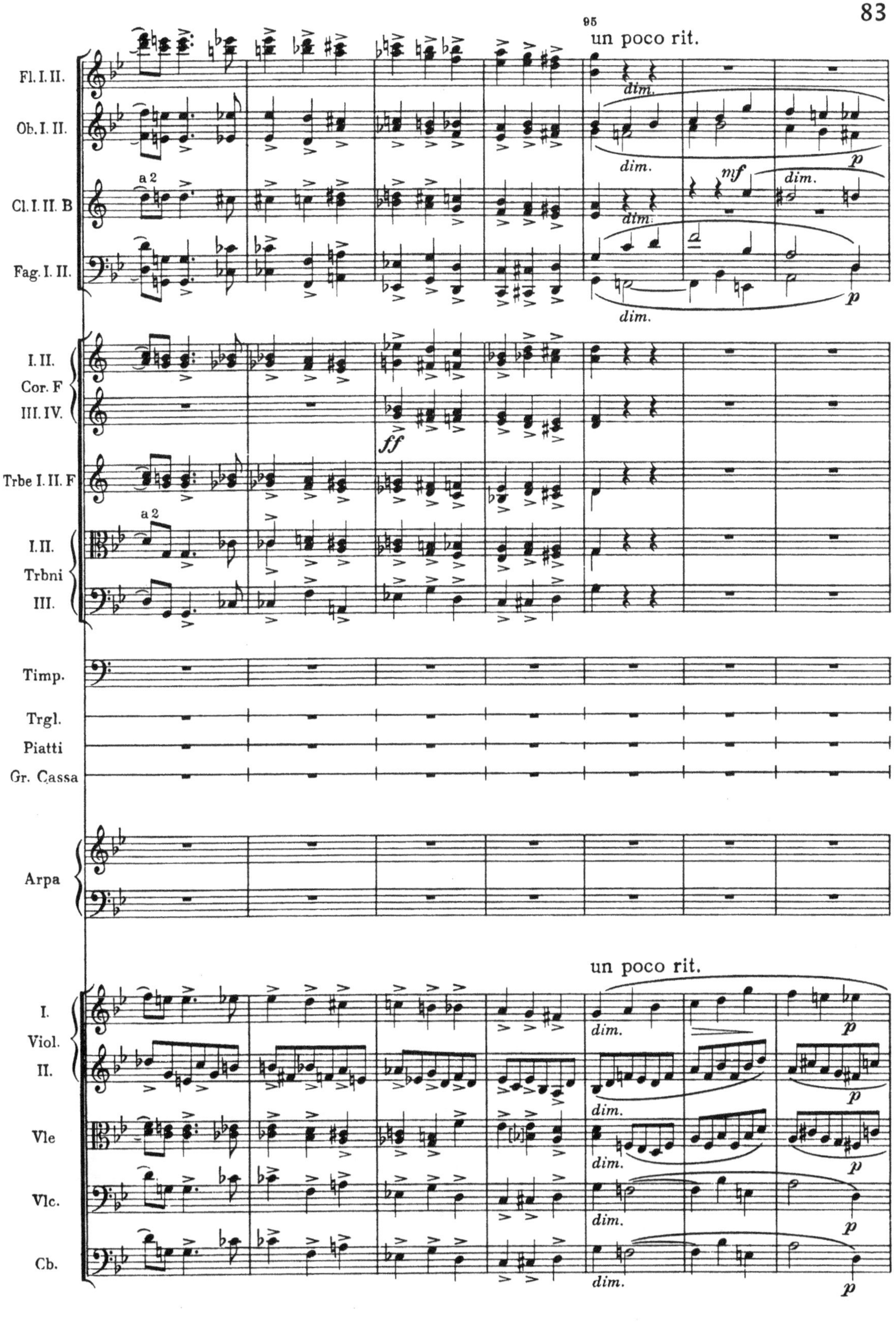
95
un poco rit.
Fl. I. II.
Ob. I. II.
Cl. I. II. B
Fag. I. II.
a 2
dim.
mf
p
I. II.
Cor. F
III. IV.
ff
Trbe I. II. F
I. II.
Trbni
III.
Timp.
Trgl.
Piatti
Gr. Cassa
Arpa
un poco rit.
I.
Viol.
II.
Vle
Vlc.
Cb.

86

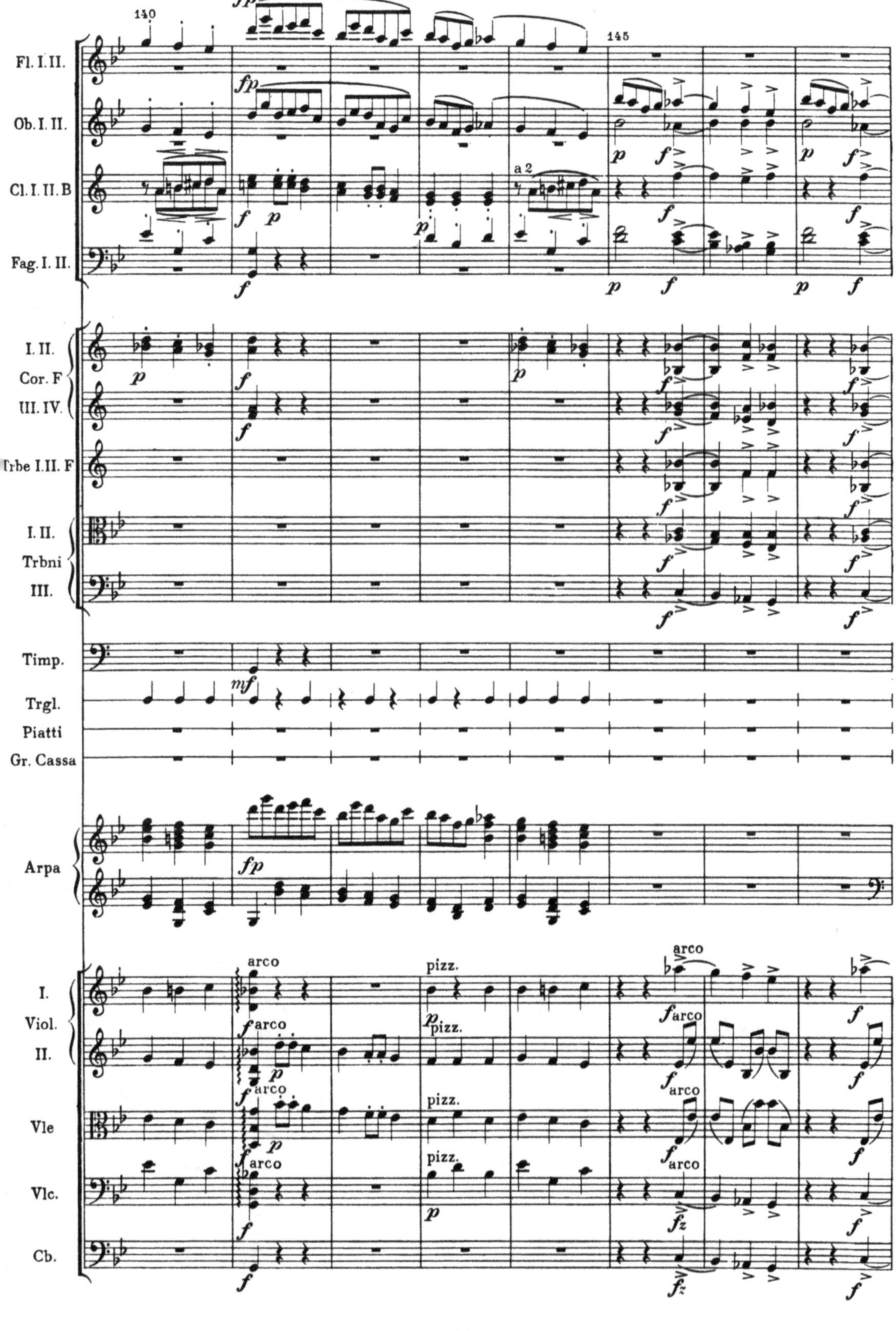
140
145
Fl. I. II.
Ob. I. II.
Cl. I. II. B
a 2
Fag. I. II.
I. II.
Cor. F
III. IV.
Trbe I. II. F
I. II.
Trbni
III.
Timp.
Trgl.
Piatti
Gr. Cassa
Arpa
I.
Viol.
II.
Vle
Vlc.
Cb.
arco
pizz.

90

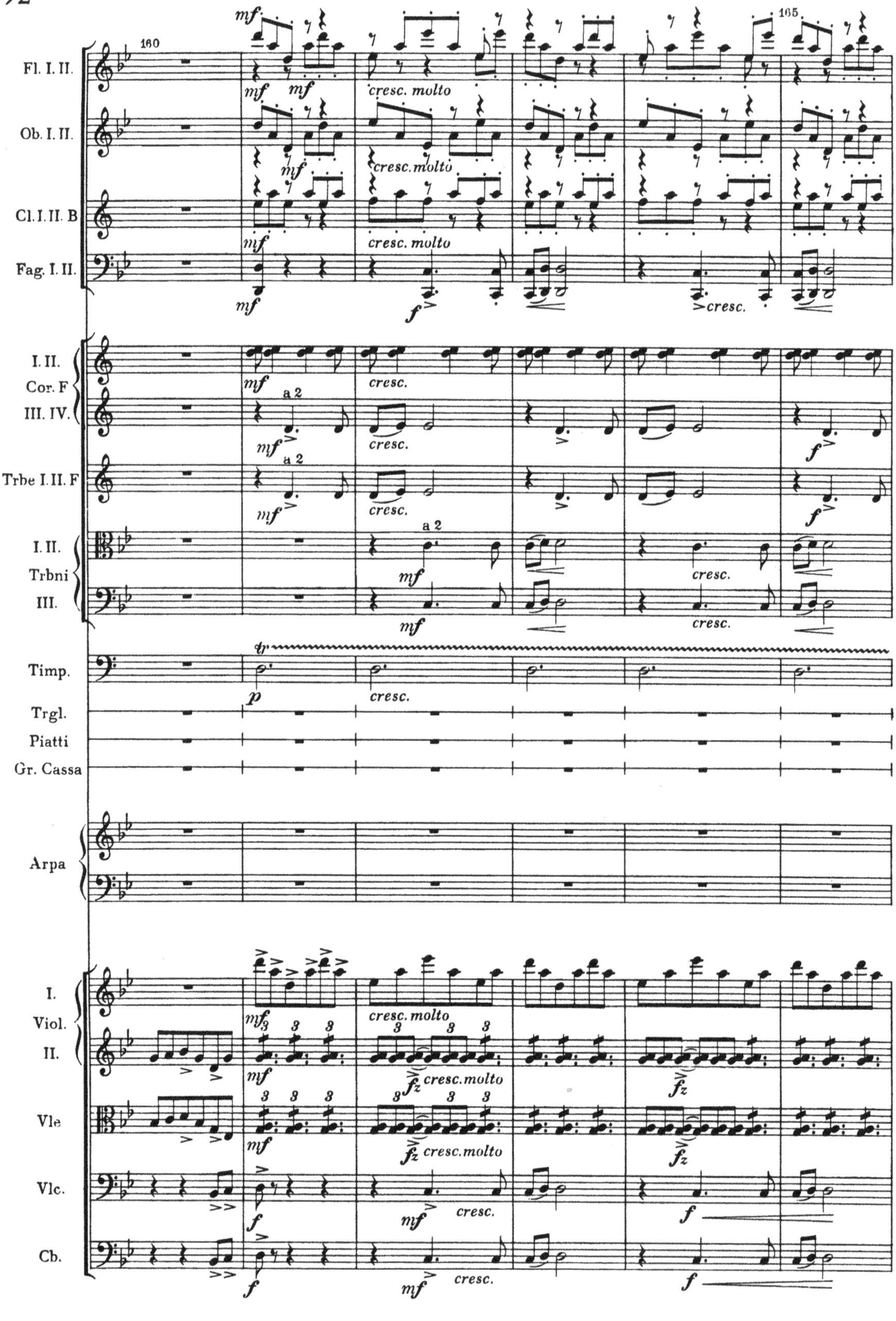
160
165
Fl. I. II.
Ob. I. II.
Cl. I. II. B
Fag. I. II.
I. II.
Cor. F
III. IV.
Trbe I. II. F
I. II.
Trbni
III.
Timp.
Trgl.
Piatti
Gr. Cassa
Arpa
I.
Viol.
II.
Vle
Vlc.
Cb.
mf
cresc. molto
cresc.
a 2
f
p
fz
tr

95

96

100

110

112

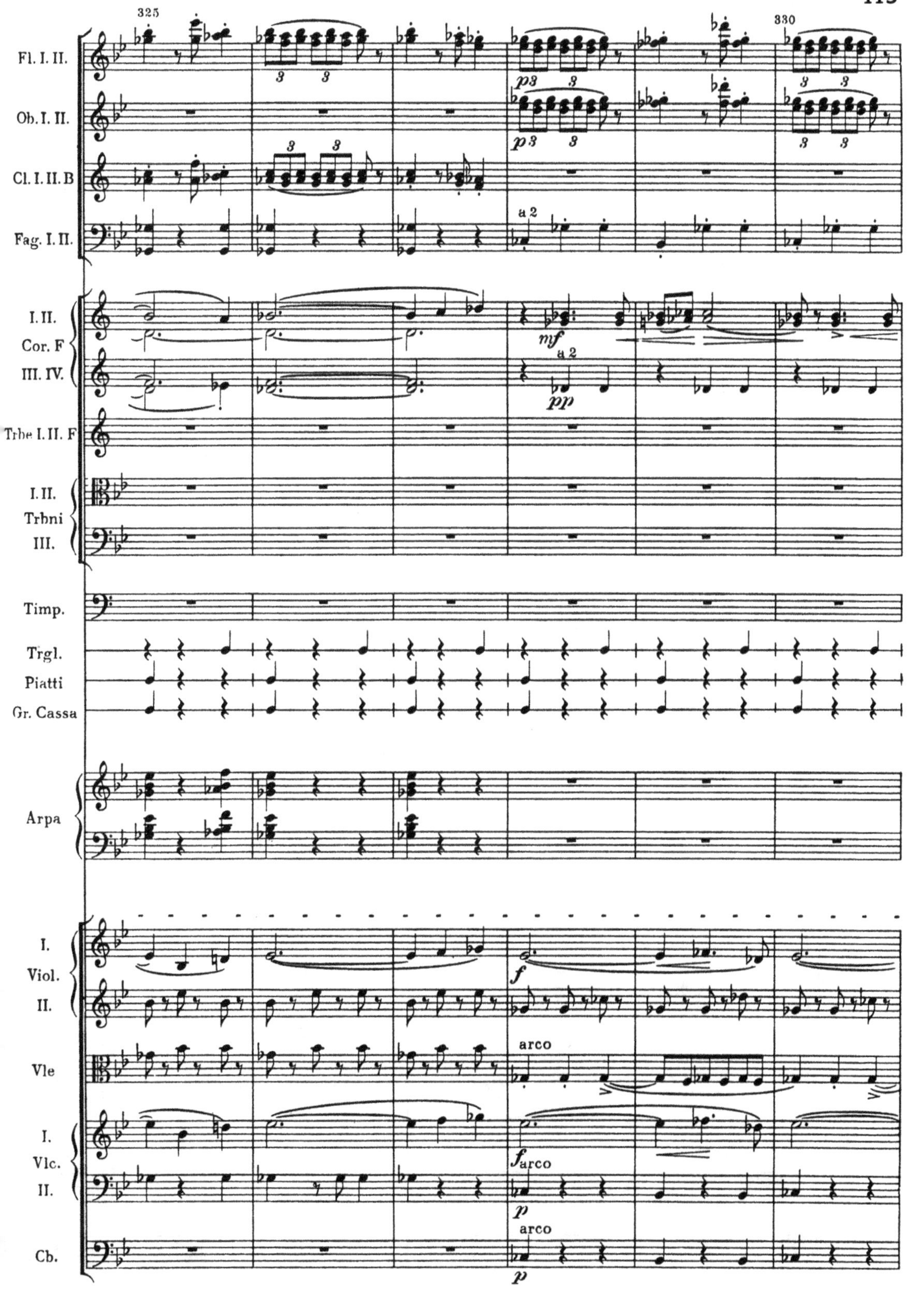
325
330
Fl. I. II.
Ob. I. II.
Cl. I. II. B
Fag. I. II.
a 2
I. II.
Cor. F
III. IV.
Trbe I. II. F
I. II.
Trbni
III.
Timp.
Trgl.
Piatti
Gr. Cassa
Arpa
I.
Viol.
II.
Vle
arco
I.
Vlc.
II.
arco
Cb.

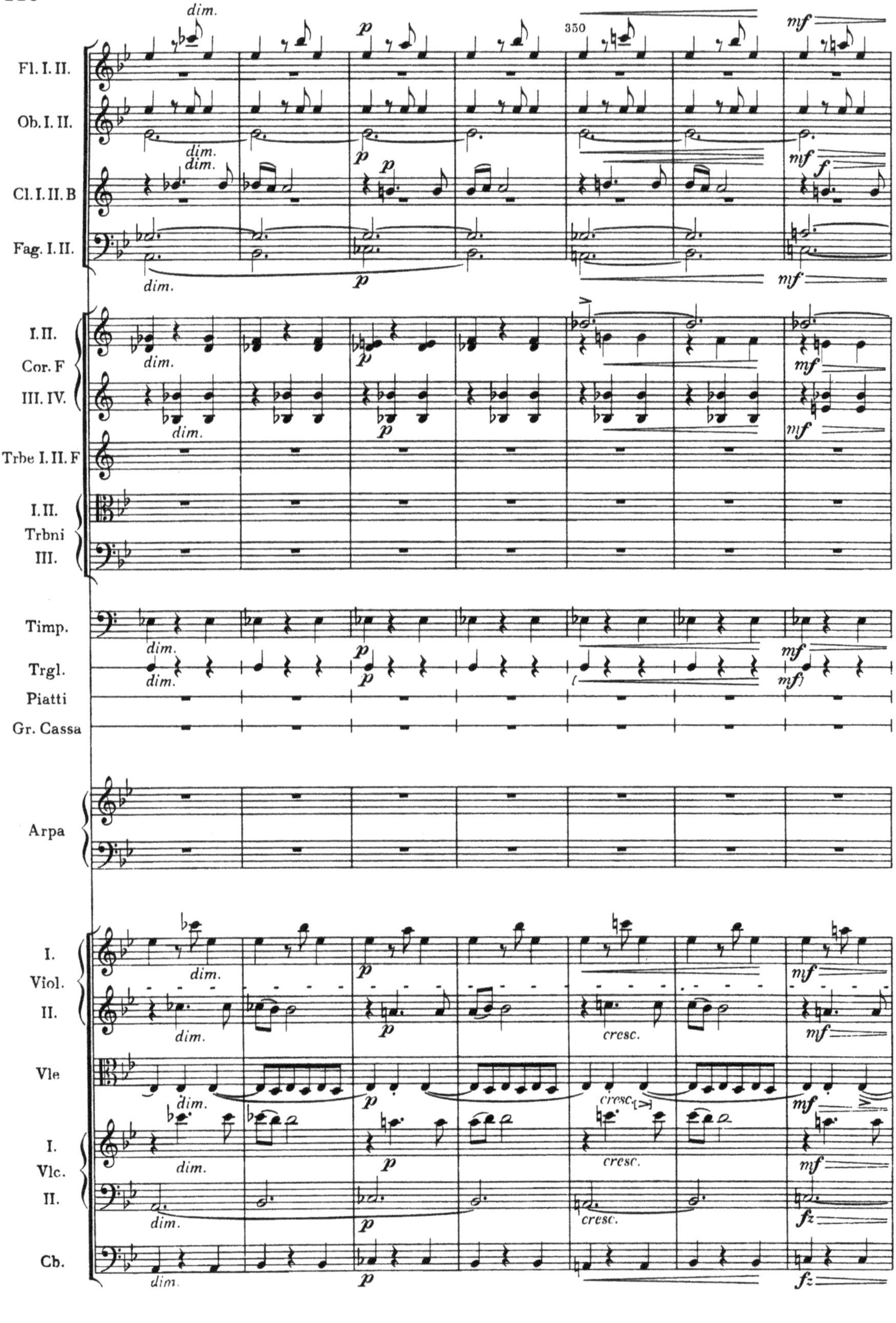

dim.
p
350
mf
Fl. I. II.
Ob. I. II.
Cl. I. II. B
Fag. I. II.
I. II.
Cor. F
III. IV.
Trbe I. II. F
I. II.
Trbni
III.
Timp.
Trgl.
Piatti
Gr. Cassa
Arpa
I.
Viol.
II.
Vle
I.
Vlc.
II.
Cb.
cresc.
f
fz

118

120

121

132

134

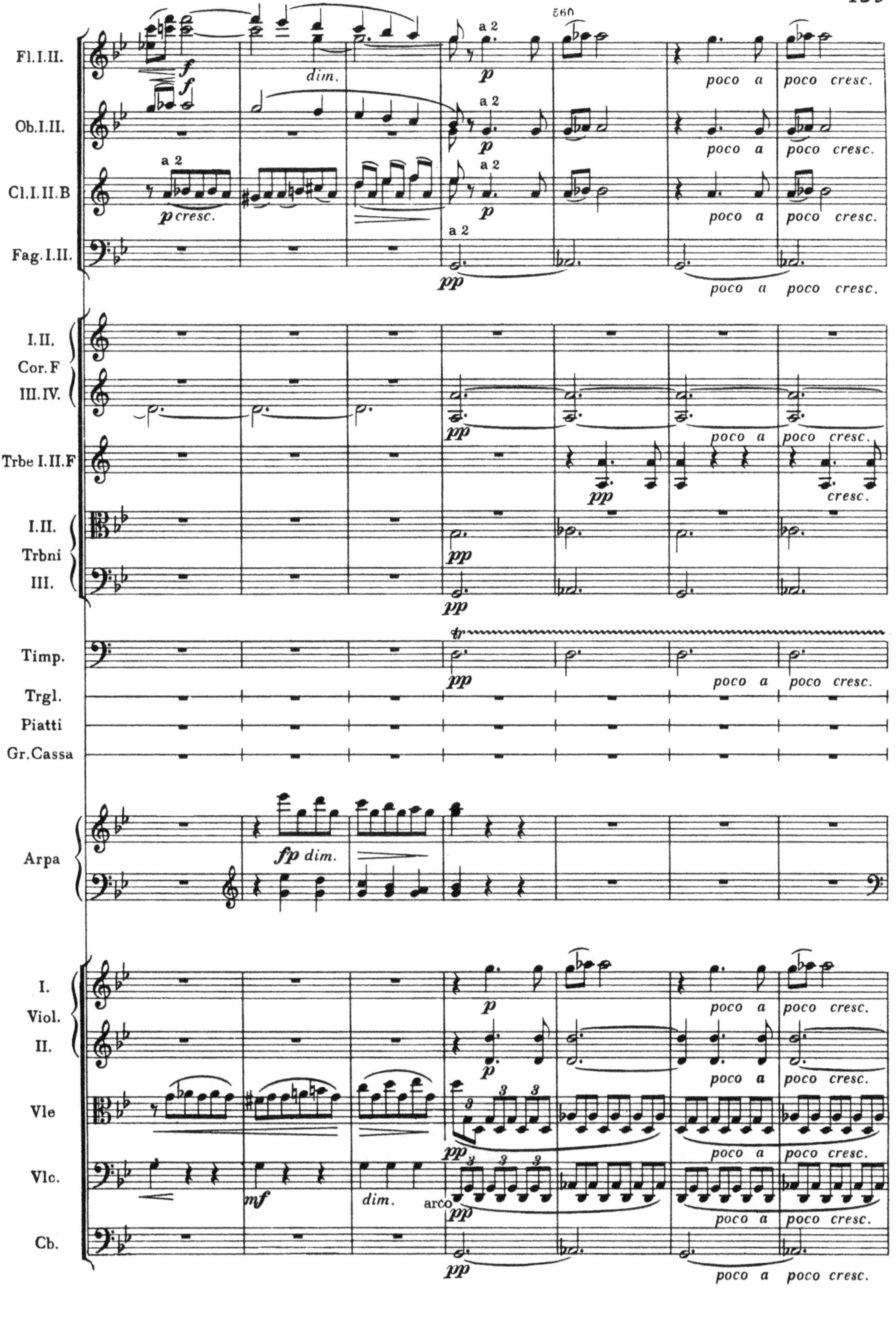

Fl.I.II.
Ob.I.II.
Cl.I.II.B
Fag.I.II.
I.II. Cor.F III.IV.
Trbe I.II.F
I.II. Trbni III.
Timp.
Trgl.
Piatti
Gr.Cassa
Arpa
I. Viol. II.
Vle
Vlc.
Cb.
a 2
dim.
p cresc.
poco a poco cresc.
fp dim.
mf
arco
pp

138

146

III

155

156

162

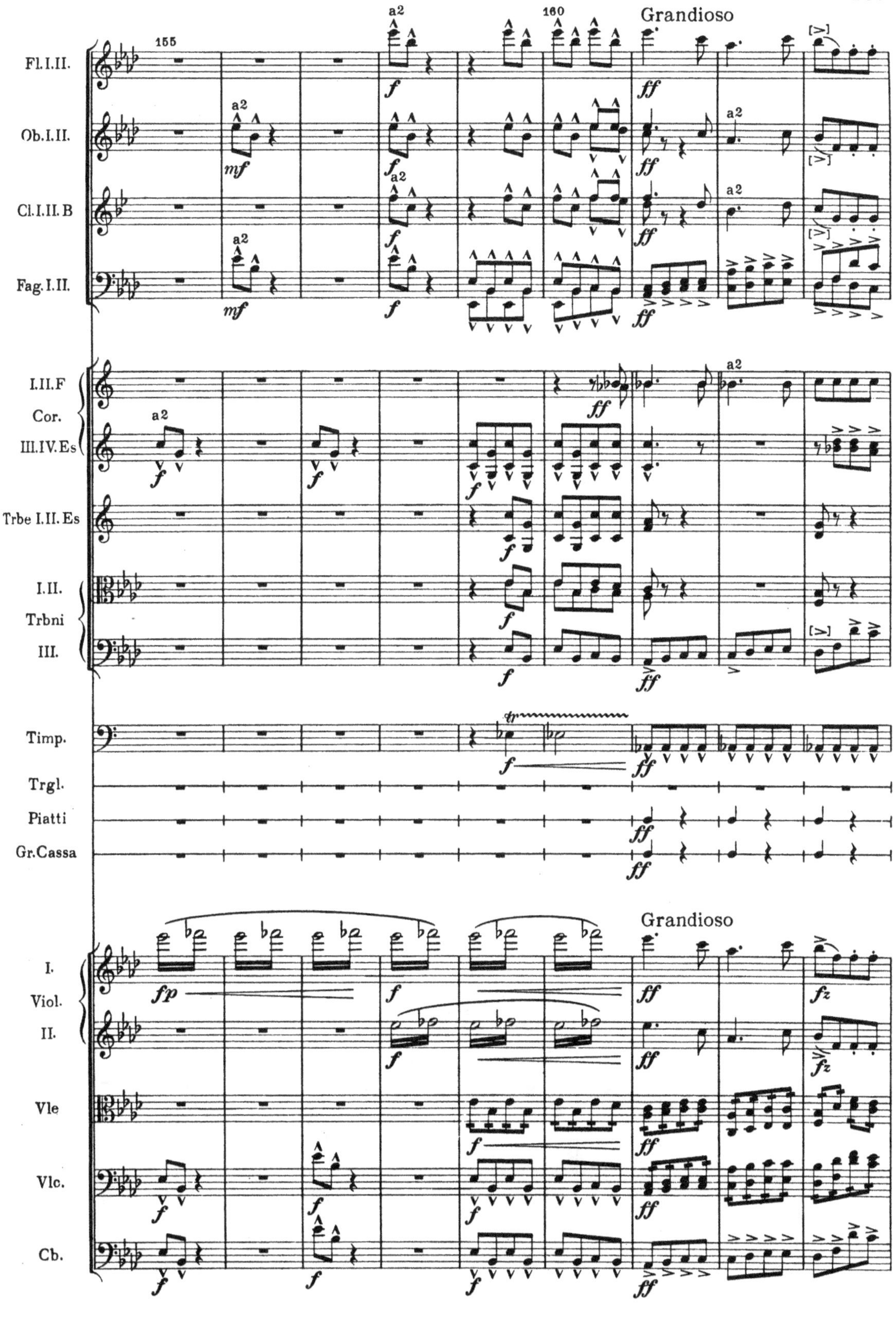
155
160
Grandioso
a2
Fl. I. II.
Ob. I. II.
Cl. I. II. B
Fag. I. II.
I. II. F
Cor.
III. IV. Es
Trbe I. II. Es
I. II.
Trbni
III.
Timp.
Trgl.
Piatti
Gr. Cassa
Grandioso
I.
Viol.
II.
Vle
Vlc.
Cb.

168

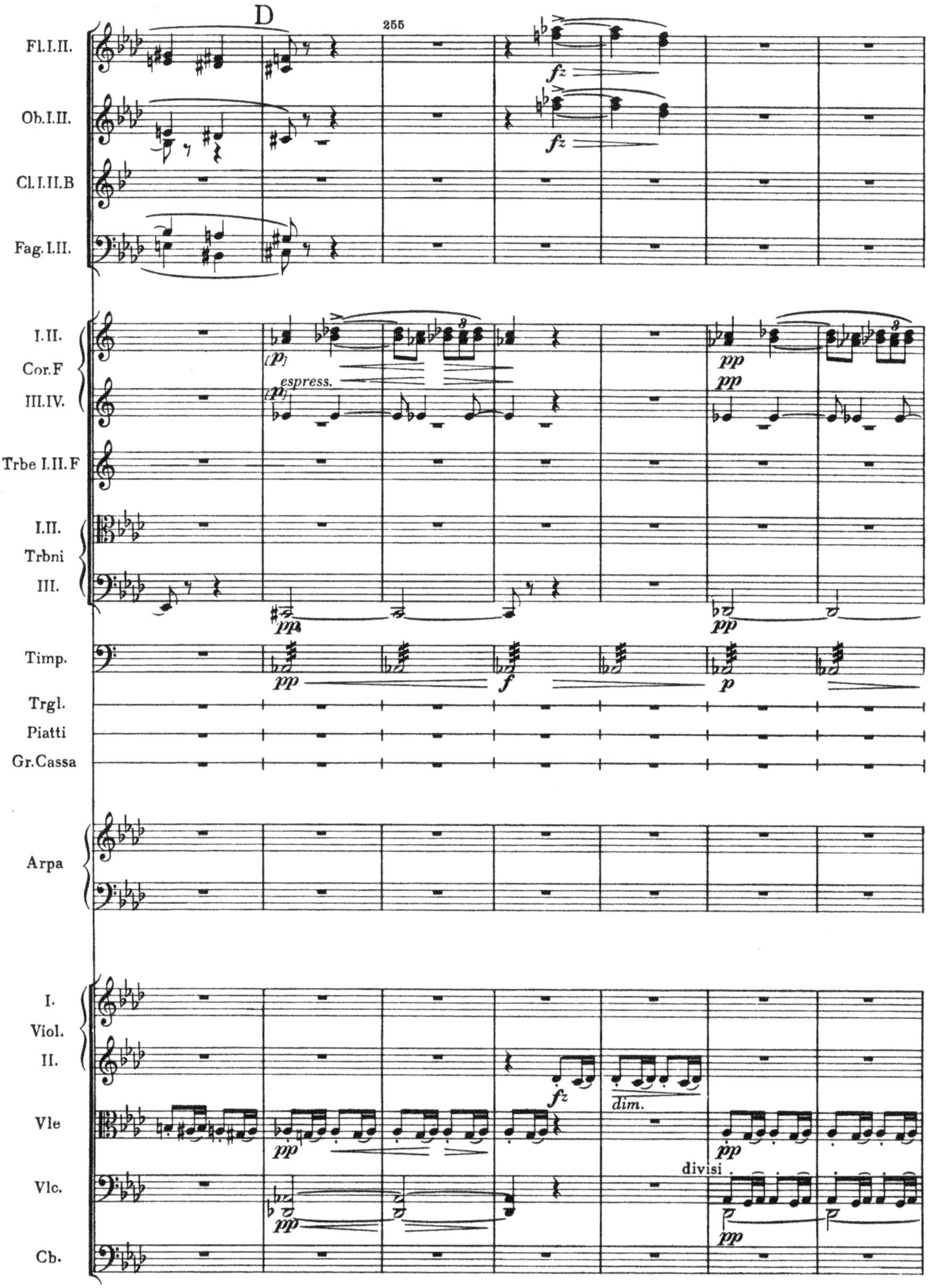
D
255
Fl.I.II.
fz
Ob.I.II.
fz
Cl.I.II.B
Fag.I.II.
I.II.
Cor.F
III.IV.
(p)
espress.
(p)
pp
pp
Trbe I.II.F
I.II.
Trbni
III.
pp
pp
Timp.
pp
f
p
Trgl.
Piatti
Gr.Cassa
Arpa
I.
Viol.
II.
fz
dim.
Vle
pp
pp
Vlc.
divisi
pp
pp
Cb.

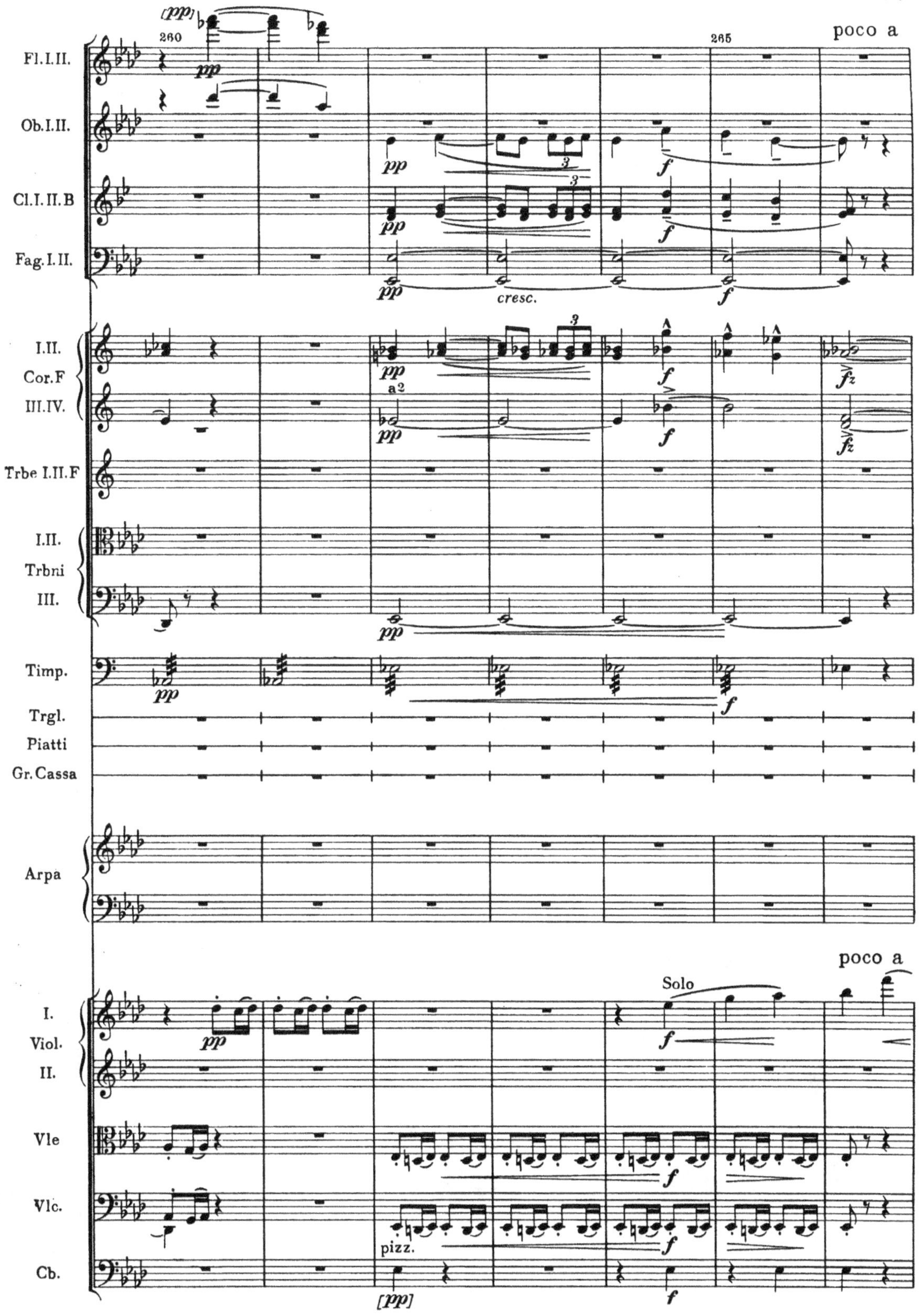
Fl.I.II.
Ob.I.II.
Cl.I.II.B
Fag.I.II.
I.II.
Cor.F
III.IV.
Trbe I.II.F
I.II.
Trbni
III.
Timp.
Trgl.
Piatti
Gr.Cassa
Arpa
I.
Viol.
II.
Vle
Vlc.
Cb.
260
265
poco a
cresc.
a2
Solo
pizz.
poco a

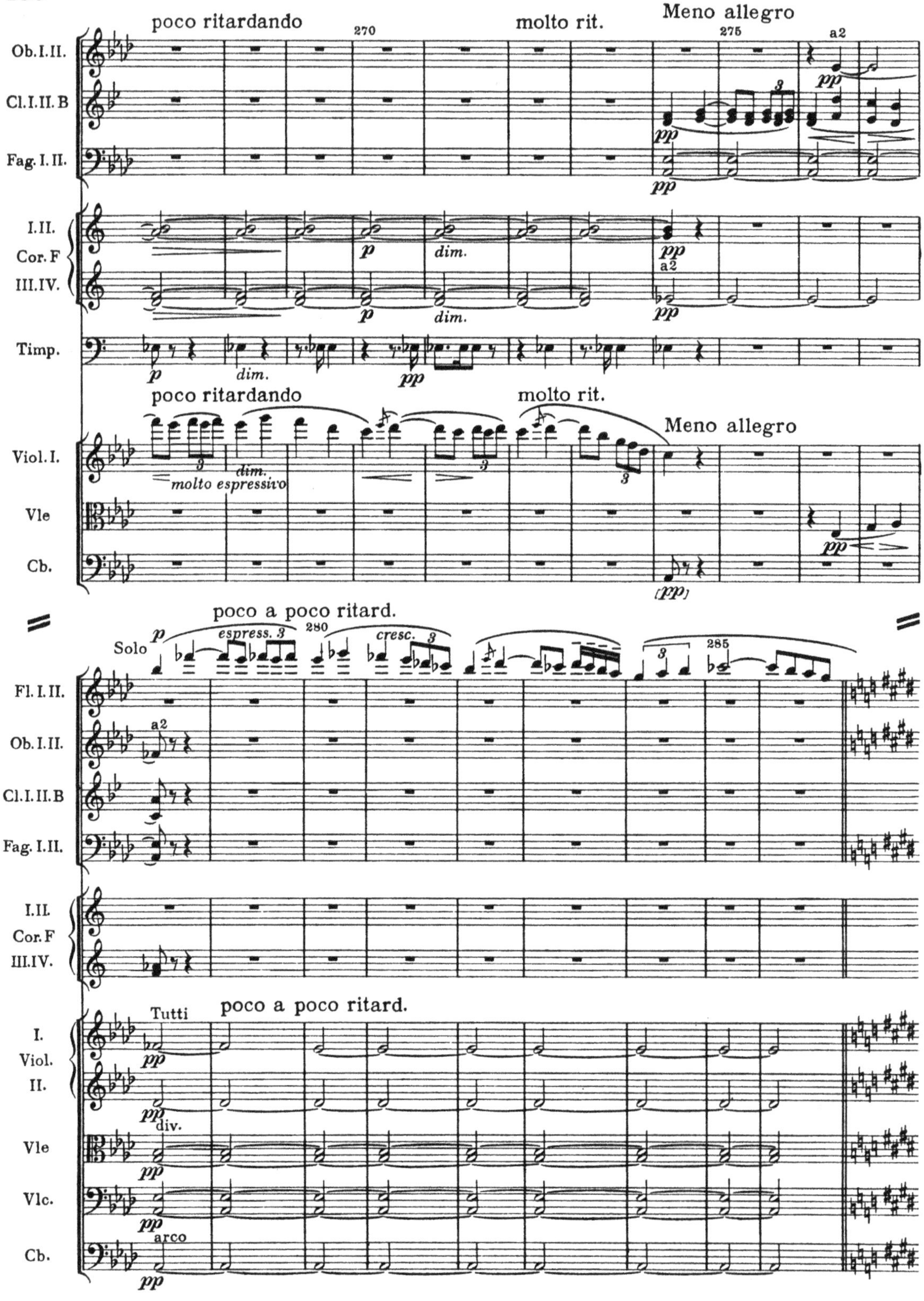
poco ritardando
molto rit.
Meno allegro
Ob. I. II.
Cl. I. II. B
Fag. I. II.
I. II. Cor. F III. IV.
Timp.
Viol. I.
Vle
Cb.
molto espressivo
dim.
a2
poco a poco ritard.
Solo
espress.
cresc.
Fl. I. II.
Tutti
div.
arco
Viol. I. II.
Vlc.

182

184

188

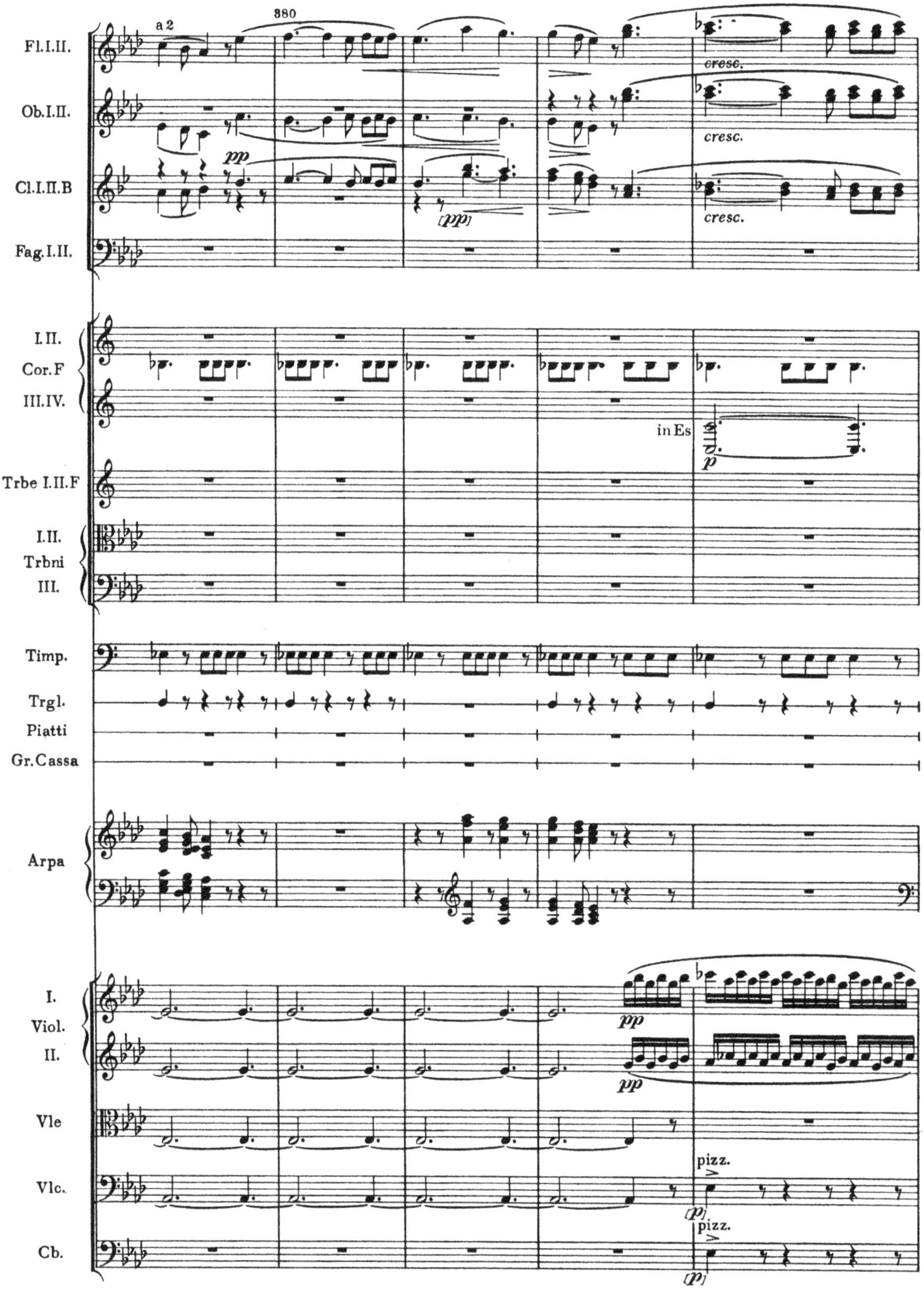
880
a 2
Fl.I.II.
Ob.I.II.
Cl.I.II.B
Fag.I.II.
I.II.
Cor.F
III.IV.
in Es
Trbe I.II.F
I.II.
Trbni
III.
Timp.
Trgl.
Piatti
Gr.Cassa
Arpa
I.
Viol.
II.
Vle
Vlc.
Cb.
pp
[pp]
cresc.
cresc.
cresc.
p
pp
pp
pizz.
[p]
pizz.
[p]

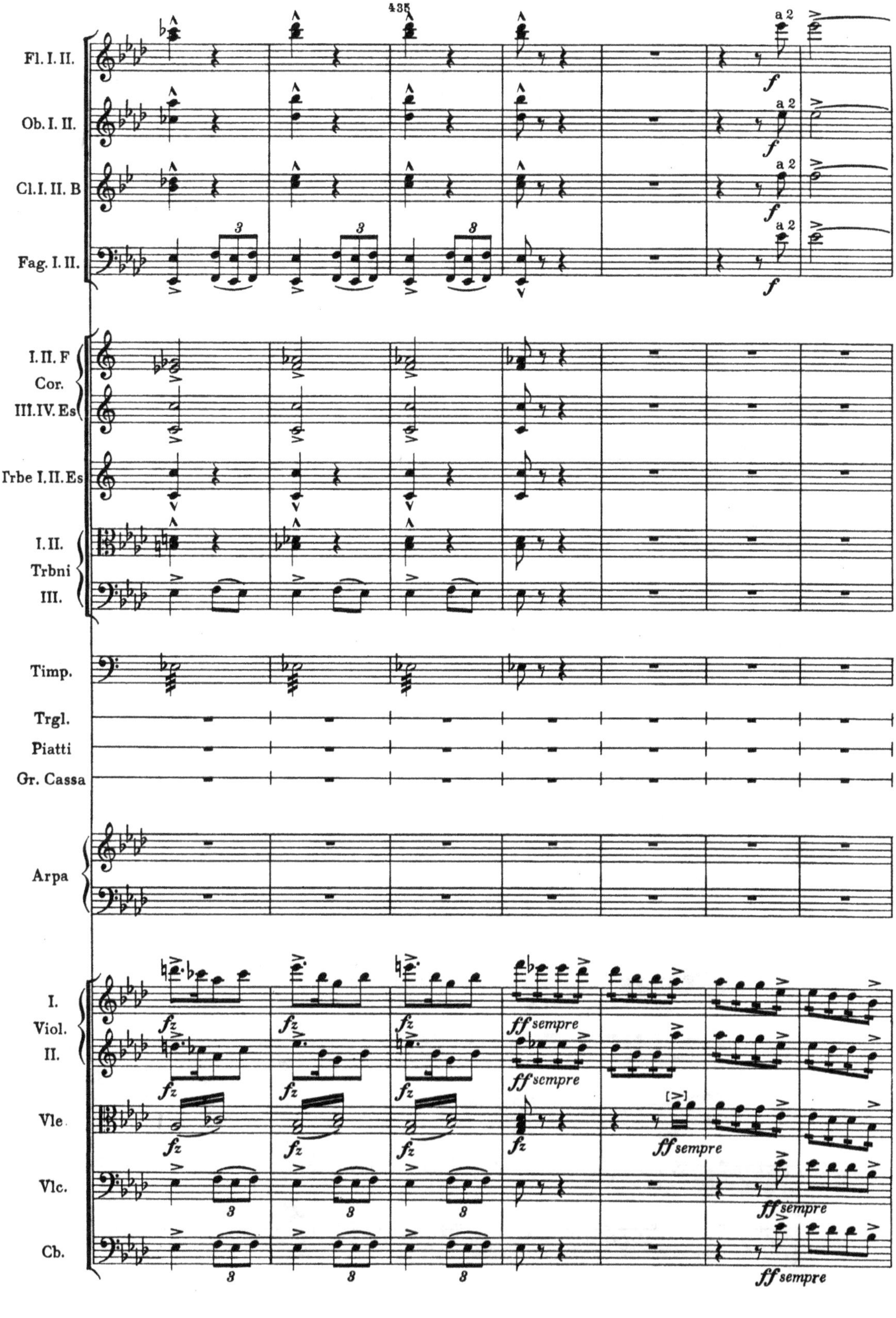
435
Fl. I. II.
Ob. I. II.
Cl. I. II. B
Fag. I. II.
a 2
f
I. II. F
Cor.
III. IV. Es
Trbe I. II. Es
I. II.
Trbni
III.
Timp.
Trgl.
Piatti
Gr. Cassa
Arpa
I.
Viol.
II.
Vle
Vlc.
Cb.
fz
ff sempre

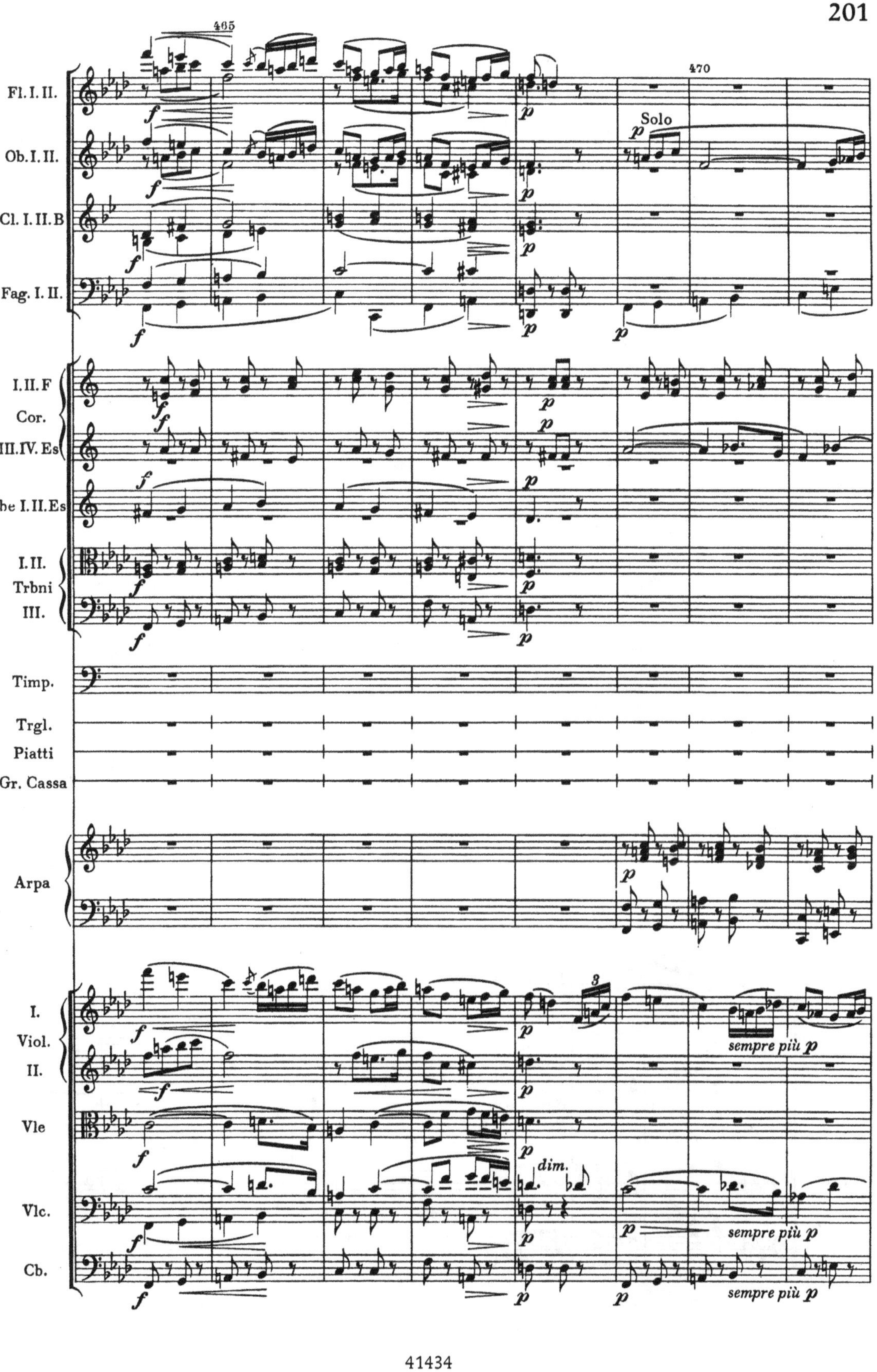
465
470
Fl. I. II.
Ob. I. II.
Solo
Cl. I. II. B
Fag. I. II.
I. II. F
Cor.
III. IV. Es
Trbe I. II. Es
I. II.
Trbni
III.
Timp.
Trgl.
Piatti
Gr. Cassa
Arpa
I.
Viol.
II.
Vle
Vlc.
Cb.
dim.
sempre più p
sempre più p
sempre più p

204

207

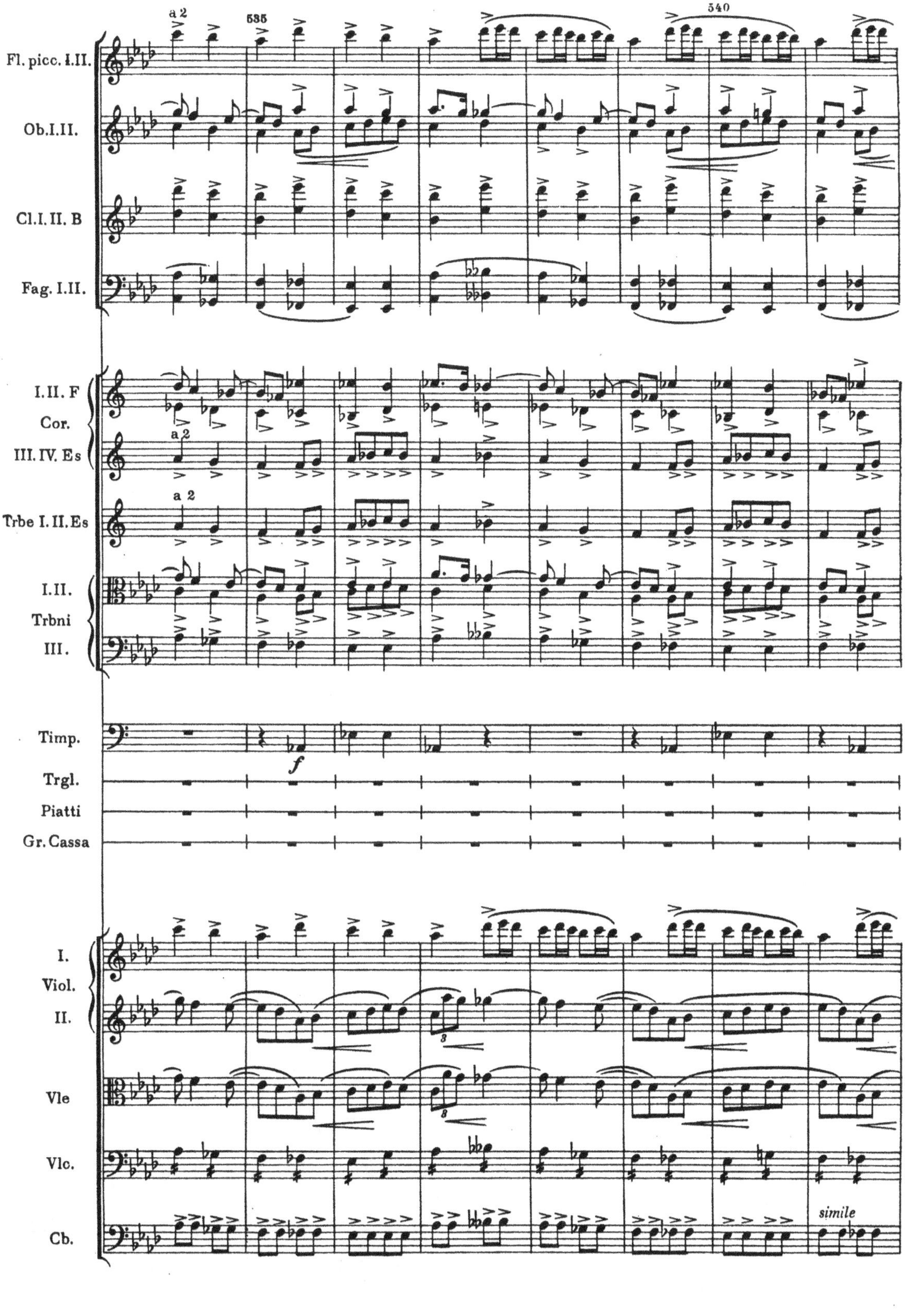
a 2
535
540
Fl. picc. I.II.
Ob.I.II.
Cl.I.II. B
Fag. I.II.
I.II. F
Cor.
III.IV. Es
a 2
a 2
Trbe I.II.Es
I.II.
Trbni
III.
Timp.
f
Trgl.
Piatti
Gr.Cassa
I.
Viol.
II.
3
Vle
3
Vlc.
Cb.
simile

214

www.ingramcontent.com/pod-product-compliance
Lightning Source LLC
Chambersburg PA
CBHW080501110426
42742CB00017B/2965